OOT THE WINDAE

Memories of a childhood in Glasgow

OOT THE WINDAE

Aboard my Tramcar of Rhyme

David Reilly

Memories of a childhood in Glasgow

LINDSAY
PUBLICATIONS

First Published in 2000 by
Lindsay Publications
Glasgow G14 9NP

© 2000 David Reilly

E-mail: david@ootthewindae.com

British Library Cataloguing-in-Publication Data
A Catalogue record for this book is available from the British Library

ISBN 1 898169 24 1

Layout and design by Eric Mitchell

Printed and bound in Scotland by Bell & Bain Limited, Glasgow

Acknowledgements

When you were a child and you were given something by a family friend or a total stranger, before you had a chance to open your mouth your mother would cry: "*What do you say?!*" "Thanks."

I am grateful to the people who made this book possible.

Malcolm Darby's *Journey through my childhood* gave me the idea to write about my childhood in poetic form.

Richard Brady, my former boss, gave me the motivation and the inspiration to actually put my thoughts into words.

My dear friend and colleague Roy Hubbard who suggested a series of self-contained poems as opposed to continuous verse which was my original thought. I thank him for his patience and wisdom in his role of editor for as soon as I had finished a piece it was on his desk for inspection.

I thank the girls in the office Jane, Linda, Charlene, Beena, Pat, Jan and Maxine whom I used as guinea pigs and presented them with my stories to watch their reaction and listen to their comments.

To Donald MacDonald of Lindsay Publications who took the time to listen to me and to read my stories. Having the faith in me and my book and to put his hand in his pocket for an unknown poet and author is quite exceptional in todays' business world.

To Carl Dineen who took my work from a series of uncoordinated poems and pictures and helped me transform them into this book. Well done Carl and many thanks.

To George Burt of *The Gen* who is unaware of how much encouragement he gave me from his first sighting of a couple of poems to the finished article. He had me on cloud nine and kept me there – wonderful motivation.

To all the neighbours, boys and girls of Gretna Street and the surrounding streets who all contributed to a very happy childhood.

My final, but perhaps biggest, thanks to my parents who brought up five boys in the East End of Glasgow and who gave us a good and solid grounding for future life.

DAVID REILLY
August, 2000

The photographs and illustrations used in the book are by courtesy of:

The author for pages 12, 17, 23, 38, 47, 65, 69, 81, 82, 92 and cover.
Alan Kane of Gryffe Fine Arts, the Savoy Centre, Glasgow for page 29.
The Mitchell Library, Glasgow for pages 15, 26, 28, 31, 32, 60, 73, 74, 84, 85.
Winnie Tyrell of the Glasgow Museums for pages 24, 30, 41, 44, 58, 68.
The McDonald collection for pages 45, 46.
W Parr for page 20.
David Gray for line illustrations pages 37, 53, 67.
Eric Marlowe for line illustrations pages 50, 55, 57, 89.

Footnote

Sadly Roy Hubbard died before I had produced the final project. My deepest sympathies go to his wife Phyll, son Andrew and daughter Amanda and again thank them for Roy's valued input to my book.

Foreword

When I was approached by a very dear friend about writing this piece I nearly fell out with him. I was up to my neck in my own testimonial dinner and having several other projects in hand, the last thing I needed was to sit down and read poetry. I am glad I did.

I left Glasgow in 1956, and have spent most of my life working and living in England, but as soon as I opened this book I was transported back to my childhood, back to the deepest recesses of my memory, to areas that I would possibly never have thought of revisiting.

I could identify with most of the situations described, from playing 'records' with the wee tanner ball to going the messages – sadly I could also recount losing childhood friends.

Although this book is based in Glasgow it could be written about any big city and I am sure anyone who lived throughout the fifties and sixties will be able to relate to the stories so vividly contained herein.

David Reilly has developed a unique style of writing which is easy to read and ponder over as well as being very entertaining. It wasn't until I had finished reading did I realise that I had just read a poetry book. I am looking forward to the sequel.

FRANK McLINTOCK, MBE

Frank McLintock

Dedication

To my father whom I was named after and miss far more
than ever I thought possible.

And my father-in-law John Curran, the kindest, most
gentle man you could ever wish to meet.

When I pass away and go to the other side
if there's a boozers and a bookies these two I'm sure to find.

Contents

THE TRAMCAR OF RHYME

Allow me to take you into my past
back to my childhood that happened so fast
and to help us on this journey in time
we'll climb aboard my tramcar of rhyme
we will take it down to memory lane
turn left at Glasgow when I was a wean
so cast away doubts and open your mind
and savour the pleasure I'm sure you'll find

Born after the war and a baby boomer
of married parents despite the rumour
my story is told in Glasgow's east end
in the fifties and sixties when we set the trend
it is based on observations and anecdotes
from hundreds of hastily scribbled notes
you will find my story both funny and sad
my growing up days when I was a lad

I want to remind all you fifty pluses
about our tramrides before there was buses
there is no need for the three ha'penny fare
as the rhythm of the tram will take you there
we will go back to when we were nippers
long before the pipe and slippers
we'll cross the bridge of generation
no matter creed or colour or political persuasion

I want to tell the kids of today
what it was like to go out and play
and what it was like before the telly
or to go to bed on an empty belly
but I also want them to share in the fun
of the all the games played in the sun
I would like to teach them a few of our tricks
when we shared a lolly so we all had licks

So allow my childhood's observation
to paint pictures in your imagination
and let us revisit those bygone days
when the sun shone brighter through the haze
let me take your hand and we'll go together
down through the years to the sunny weather
for in my memory the sun always shines
so all aboard my tramcar of rhymes

David, Michael and Baby Jim in the pram – 1952

THE FLITTING

The five of us slept in that single end
in a ground floor flat let from a friend
it was overrun with rats and mice
who were always complaining about the lice
the outside toilet was forever blocked
its door always open and never locked
completely different from those upstairs
clean and tidy with newspaper in squares

This was the summer of fifty three
I was four years old and not a pick on me
we just had a party with rest of the nation
celebrating the Queen's coronation
linen covered tables round all the backs
laden with sandwiches and various snacks
we all got sweeties in a commemorative tin
which mothers for years put their buttons in

A letter arrived although it was late
about a bigger house on a newer estate
the corporation wanted us to view
a two bedroomed flat with an inside loo
we'd been on the waiting list for years
and mother couldn't hide her tears
located somewhere in the back of beyond
the place of my childhood and memories fond

There were no houses just rows of flats
each with their own welcome mats
no rats or mice or single ends
no outside toilets to share with friends
our two bedrooms looked onto the street
as did the bathroom with its enamel suite
the living room and scullery faced the rear
the clothes lines and middens were located here

Came the big day when we had to flit
all our belongings moved bit by bit
on the back of a lorry that carried coal
to take us away from this filthy hole
Mother took the tram the number nine
my two wee brothers straggling behind
me and my Dad went on the lorry
leaving the rats without saying sorry

I was in the front holding our cat
we called it Darkie as black as your hat
there was no prejudice or racial abuse
this was the name we called the puss
I wondered if she would like the place
with no rats or mice for her to chase
but there was plenty of other mogs
being chased in turn by the local dogs

After a short journey we arrived in the street
and out came the neighbours for us to meet
I never heard the rallying call
for we had moved in in no time at all
no carpets or lino laid on the floor
just the bare boards behind every door
no washing machine no fridge or telly
no food in the cupboard for my rumbling belly

The scullery always sticks in my mind
the smallest of rooms that you can find
a back to back stove was set in the wall
and had an oven that was no good at all
on top of the stove was this gas ring
with a double burner and a toaster thing
all the mod cons the art of the day
when cooking was done you could fold it away

Below the windae there was a double sink
one for the washing and one for a drink
the back to back made the water hot
for a bath in the sink if we needed it or not
it had a pulley to hang the washing
and an empty cupboard to put our nosh in
just room for a table that would fold away
next to the bunker and Darkie's tray

We had electricity one light to a room
and only one plug for a wireless I assume
it had round pins before they went metric
that didn't matter for we had nothing electric
we'd no shades or lamps for a softer light
just a solitary bulb that burned so bright
welcome to your new home my father said
and here I would stay till the day I wed

Lawmoor Street in the Gorbals (where I was born)

15

OOT THE WINDAE

Hingin oot the windae and watch the world go by
up a close in Glesga three stories high
Ma and Da and all the weans
oot the windae until it rains
get yourself comfy for the show is free
a couple of biscuits and a wee cup of tea
a coffee for dad laced with scotch
your very original neighbourhood watch

We had a grandstand view from our top floor flat
two to each windae and still room for the cat
the street was alive and a hubbub of noise
children playing games as they didn't have toys
woman chattering at the foot of the close
going ten to the dozen to see who knew most
though men in the street were very scarce
either at work or stuck in their chairs

Regular visitors coming to and fro
each with a purpose with somewhere to go
just like the Green lady who visited the sick
delivering babies being her favourite trick
it was her who gave me my third little brother
that was four in a row and still room for another
home births were common with minimum fuss
caught out being easier than catching a bus

One welcome visitor was the man from the gas
emptying the meters for the street en masse
he'd open the meter with his special key
and emptied it's contents for all to see
he'd count the money and place in a stack
took what he needed with the rest coming back
these were normally quite prosperous times
but he kept the shillings and returned the dimes

We would wait patiently for the ice cream man
who had just got himself a brand new van
he blew a whistle before they had chimes
unlike the Capocci man of more modern times
a far cry from his three wheeler bike
an ice cream cone any vanilla flavour you like
a wafer or a nougat or an oyster shell
and a loose woodbine he would gladly sell

The tottie man would come selling fruit and veg
delivering to your doorstep anything for an edge
carrots and turnips and Brussel sprouts
new Ayrshire potatoes he proudly shouts
Fife's bananas and oranges and pears
attracting the women down the stairs
and always on a Friday he brought some fish
when I was a child a discriminating dish

When the parish priest made his weekly run
all hell was let loose if you pardon the pun
his very appearance put us all on our toes
and we pray to God he'd go past our close
he'd visit the sick the elderly and the supposed meek
and those who missed mass the previous week
he had a reputation that would never be beat
the most feared man that ever walked in our street

We looked oot the windae for most of the day
watching the workers the wifie's and children at play
we would kneel on a chair with our arms in a fold
as the events of the day would slowly unfold
we were people watchers with thoughts to share
like most in Glasgow that lived up a stair
yes we were observers from dusk to dawn
not like them nosey Parkers with their curtains drawn

My Father (right), with two of his 'drinking' buddies

18

THE COALMAN

The coal lorry came down the road
blowing profusely from its heavy load
filthy black smoke filled the air
from a leaking engine that didn't care
with one of the coalmen on its back
balancing himself as he folded a sack
his face as black as a lump of coal
totally anonymous and on the dole

He wore a waistcoat made of leather
and carried the coal in every weather
coal or nuts take your pick
ten bob a bag and always on tick
no access or visa to pay your way
it was cash or else on collection day
the price he paid was a heavy toll
a broken back for carrying coal

On the Friday night I got the job
to go and collect the peoples ten bob
for the credit was given without a fee
and the service I gave was completely free
up and down the stairs on several trips
totally dependant on customer tips
the few coppers I earned made me glad
and also the coalman who was my dad

Parkhead Cross

20

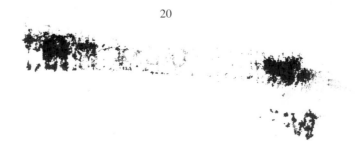

MY PAL HUGH

Let me tell you about my pal Hugh
we met at school where our friendship grew
our infant school was in Elba lane
apparently named after some place in Spain
like so many streets round Parkhead Cross
got their names from the Napoleonic wars
Hugh lived in a new tenement that shared a back
with a red sandstone building that was going black

Our class consisted of both girls and boys
you were told where to sit you had no choice
the teacher sat us together but we didn't mind
in those desks and chairs that dually combined
we had crayons and pencils and a wooden rule
and no shortage of books at our little school
for we had Dick and Dora with Nip and Fluff
and B11 jotters amongst other stuff

We hadn't met before but got on just fine
we played together all of the time
gave each other coaxies and played at tig
played at marbles mine's small his big
we were cowboys both rider and horse
smacking yourself to show who's boss
cowboys and indians with some of the others
made ourselves bleed and became blood brothers

We left the infants and went on our way
up to the primary even further away
by this time we were both aged seven
not appreciating the fun our friendship had given
we were always together like two peas in a pod
even went to church and prayed to God
he was the best pal a schoolboy could have
kidding and joking and always a laugh

But outside of school he was a different lad
he never spoke of his mum and dad
he'd rush home from school every day
very seldom stopping out to play
giving him the benefit of the doubt
maybe his parents wouldn't let him out
a couple of years later when I was nine
I would see Hugh for the very last time

Early one morning during the summer break
I was sent to the shops only half awake
we had no money for the paper and bread
so six lemonade bottles would do instead
I would read the paper before I got home
from back to front my eyes would roam
I was good at reading for a boy of my age
then I saw Hugh's photo staring out of the page

Boy killed by van the headline read
my mouth opened and I dropped the bread
he was knocked down crossing the road
by a delivery van the picture showed
I picked up the bread then ran all the way
got back home to ma and tried to say
but I couldn't speak as I was in shock
so I started to cry into her frock

I never got to know his mum or dad
and to this day it still makes me sad
I never had the chance to say goodbye
there was no mourning I don't know why
but now after all of these years
he has found a place in each of my tears
my friend as an adult I never knew
goodnight and God bless... my pal Hugh

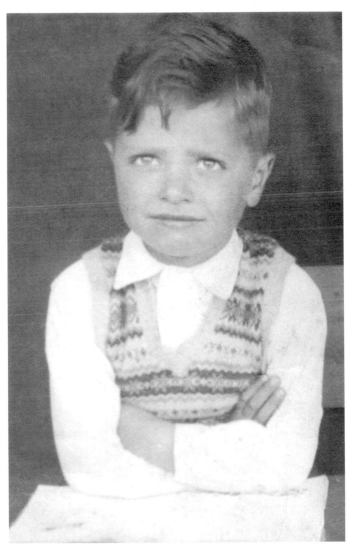

Me aged 5 at school

THE JOURNEY

By the time I was seven I had travelled the land
and I knew Glasgow like the back of my hand
I used public transport to get me around
the tram cars the trolleys and the underground
I would visit all my uncles and aunts
all over Glesga and still in short pants
down the Calton or over the Southside
completely safe either side of the Clyde

One of my favourites was my Uncle John
it was after him they nicknamed the pawn
he lived in the Gorbals quite far away
so when I went to see him I went for the day
I took the tram then I took a trolley
I considered this journey as a bit of a jolly
the trip would take just under an hour
so fasten your seatbelt and enjoy the tour

Nicholson Street in The Gorbals where Uncle John lived

I caught the tram on the London road
Dalmuir West said the destination board
now London Road was straight and wide
with tenements towering on either side
three storeys high on top of the shops
smoke belching out from chimney tops
they built these flats in rows and rows
with dozens sharing the communal close

There was a break in the pattern now and then
so to cram more in they created a pen
with wider access around the back
bulging at the seams and ready to crack
all gathered together and herded like sheep
where they counted humans to go to sleep
thousands of people occupied that space
the rats didn't want this human race

A different world down the stairs
shops are open selling their wares
the butcher the dairy the grocery stores
attracting the people through their doors
their windows covered in words of clay
telling the people what was on display
houghs and ribs and potted meat
and at these prices they couldn't be beat

I would take the tram to Bridgeton Cross
the wcc conductress always the boss
in her uniform of transport green
click click clicking her ticket machine
trying as usual to skip my fare
and often got caught but didn't care
the clippie cried *c'mon and get aff*
but I reluctantly paid my thrupenny half

I got off the tram and crossed the street
and caught the trolley always a treat
they nicknamed the trolley the silent death
it could hardly be heard above your breath
it ran on electric from overhead lines
with a silent engine that barely whines
got chucked off the bus at Gorbals cross
skipped my fair and couldn't give a toss

The Gorbals was notorious for older slums
an wi wee bits of weans arse out their bums
the lamps in the street were still lit by gas
no electric lighting for the working class
though working class was a misused phrase
in Glesga pubs where they passed their days
most out of work and in the boozers
or the other way round and just born losers

The Trolley Bus – The Silent Death

Some Gorbals streets were really great
smooth and shiny like a bed of slate
there was no gravel and no little stones
and the whole of the Gorbals car free zones
this was a natural breeding ground
where talented footballers could be found
they churned them out two for a tanner
Glesga's answer to the Copa Cabana

Another thing about these streets of slate
user friendly to the old type of skate
which could adjust to fit any size
over your shoes with straps and ties
they would come from miles around
just to skate on the smoothest of ground
pirouettes and birlies with your mates
great fun to be had on a pair of skates

And when the skates went past their best
we'd make a bogie the ultimate test
with an orange box and a plank of wood
and beer bottle tops to make it look good
we would split the skate into two
nailed to the plank a couple would do
the box on its end adding handle bars
the bottletops sparkling like colourful stars

These streets were a haven for children at play
amongst the slums so bleak and so grey
and I saw them pull all of them down
the slum clearances of Glasgow town
all along London Road to Bridgeton Cross
and through the Gorbals the people's loss
this journey couldn't be done today
for the trams and trolleys are long away

The character of the city has been lost forever
particularly the streets either side of the river
with cul-de-sacs and one way systems
if you blink going past your sure to miss them
the motorways and fly-overs travelled at pace
have made the city a far smaller place
and all the districts once clearly defined
are joined together on a motorway sign

Preparing for the Clearance

Bridgeton Cross

Gorbals Cross

THE CANDYMAN

He came from the south in his pony and trap
like Gabby Hayes a most memorable chap
he'd come into the street cracking his whip
catching his horse with the lightest of tip
and all the kids would form a queue
like Noah's Ark two by two
a penny a ride around the block
the nearest to a stagecoach we ever got

He was a popular visitor to east end streets
and always came with a bag of sweets
it didn't matter if you hadn't the penny
you still got a sweet he brought that many
I wonder today how he earned a living
or if this was charity that he was giving
who was that man this mysterious stranger
we called the Candyman our Lone Ranger

THE RAGMAN

He gave you fair warning whenever he came
though the tune he played was never the same
in a neighbouring street a bugler played
and it wasn't the lifeboys or boys' brigade
all the young mothers gripped with fear
as this dreaded bugler came ever near
tis the ragman playing a chordless tune
the bedraggled Pied Piper of Glesga toon

Came into our street pushing his cart
didn't need a horse he played that part
his old brown case was full of toys
like Santa's grotto to the girls and boys
paint sets and crayons and coloured chalk
to create a design on your whipping top
spud guns and peashooters and catapult slings
the toys of war the ragman brings

The Boys' Brigade on Parade

The Ragman – The Pied Piper of Glesga Toon

Took out a Woodbine the last of his fags
then he bellowed *toys for rags*
last blast on the bugle and then he'd hush
lit up and waited for the expected rush
the kids in the street would all go mad
looking for rags from their mum and dad
in all the cupboards throughout the rooms
a handful of rags for a couple of balloons

With great anticipation they stood in line
eyes fixed on the ragman all of the time
no pounds or ounces of imperial measure
just a bundle of rags for unlimited treasure
though I could only stand and stare
we never seemed to have rags to spare
now looking back and assessing the facts
all of our rags were on our backs

THE SHOP

Whilst we were either cowboys or cops
the girls busied themselves playing at shops
with mothers best tablecloth or linen sheet
they'd set out their stalls down in the street
using the kerb that once held rails
as the counter to put up their scales
alongside a till or a moneybox
with dirt from the garden providing their stocks

With an old spoon they would dig the soil
a heap of dirt a reward for their toil
filling boxes and tins and paper pokes
paying no attention to our cissy jokes
they'd fill each container full of dirt
being careful not to dirty their skirt
then wash their hands with utmost pride
our store is open come inside

A packet of soap powder came in an Oxydol box
a make believe detergent to wash out your socks
a tin of spaghetti made an earthy food
with a couple of worms to make it look good
there was chocolate and tablet and macaroon bars
and chucky stone sweeties in old jeely jars
sauce bottles with water straight from the sink
mixed with licorice made a sugarolli drink

They had no money with which to pass
so the next best thing was to deal in glass
each piece of glass had a value to trade
clear glass being common and the lowest grade
coloured glass from bottles that once held wine
was valued more and next in line
then came porcelain from a shattered mug
and terracotta earthenware from a broken jug

But the glass that was most valued in kind
was white china which was difficult to find
particularly if there was a rim of gold
worth a fortune or so I was told
though the broken glass had no value as such
and the goods on sale just as much
what was priceless was the values taught
in the money spent and the bargain bought

(Picture reproduced courtesy of Procter & Gamble)

THE WATCHIE

Now and again the street got relaid
by a load of Paddy's who were poorly paid
the muscular men on the pneumatic drill
digging the street gave the woman a thrill
the biceps bulging from a dirty vest
which failed to hide their hairy chest
they hung out the windae and never spoke
quite uncommon for our woman folk

Then came the machine that laid the tar
carefully avoiding a solitary car
the street was laid one side at a time
and straight as a die no need for a line
and there was no need for a traffic light
although the road was narrow and access tight
for traffic at this time was very sparse
there were very few lorries and even fewer cars

The steamroller would follow them up
puffing and panting Putt Putt Putt
this massive machine showed amazing grace
as it trundled slowly at walking pace
levelling completely every bump and crack
with a one front wheel and two at the back
I now understand why enthusiasts dream
of this giant workhorse running on steam

You could make a hatchet if you were quick
with an old tin can at the end of a stick
you would place the can under a wheel
and watch it flatten under ten ton of steel
then finally on the top of the tar
they scattered the gravel near and far
the steamroller then made a final run
finished for the day a job well done

The men went home and off to their pit
on came the watchie to look after their kit
his first job at night was to light the lights
to protect the machines on winter nights
he then loaded his brazier full of coke
and lit up his pipe and had a smoke
he waited patiently for the fire to catch
put his hand down his trousers and had a good scratch

The fire was glowing time for a brew
with no mod cons he knew what to do
no electric kettle no pot nor pan
on top of the fire he boiled his can
his sugar and tea came in a little brass tin
a lid at each end and separated within
poured milk from a bottle that once held scotch
then checked the time on his pocket watch

The fire was a magnet on a winter's night
like moths to a lamp that was burning bright
we all snuggled up in the watchies hut
very late at night when all was shut
the watchman made the perfect host
he opened a loaf and we all made toast
sadly if the watchman did this today
PC would come and take him away

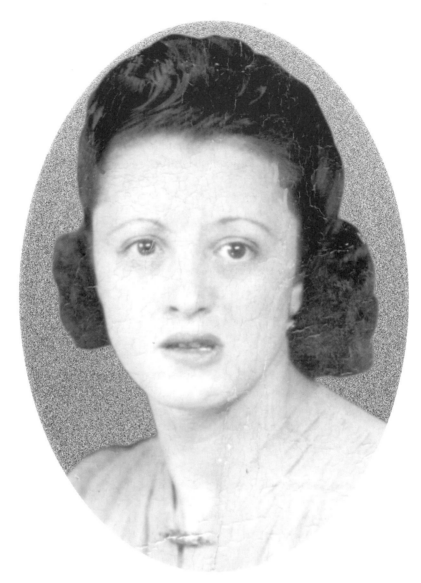

My Mother in her early twenties

THE HOME

I woke up one morning to my mothers sob
my father had just started another job
she was crying and moaning about a sore head
with the pain so severe she had to stay in bed
I was the oldest of our family of four
I had three little brothers and then one more
there was David Michael Jim and Pat
and Wee Alex to come shortly after that

With mother unwell I had to stay off school
this was the exception and not the rule
I was only eight but I was smart for my age
and very responsible as you may gauge
so I got the two eldest out of their bed
washed and dressed and their faces fed
took them to school then hurried hame
just in time to feed the wean

It may have taken a couple of hours
to go to the shop and do the chores
like taking the ashes down to the bin
and tidying the house as clean as a pin
by mid-morning she was still no better
a couple of aspirin was all I could get her
her head was still pounding and she started to cry
but an eight year old's mother would never die

Her crying had receded to a whimpering moan
an occasional sigh followed a painful groan
it was becoming obvious she was getting worse
and needed a doctor or even a nurse
she was sweating heavily and was violently sick
I knew I had to do something and do it quick
so I ran to a neighbour and prayed she was home
the only person I knew that owned a phone

She called the Doctor on behalf of my mother
then took me home to look after my brother
she mopped her brow until the doctor came
and almost immediately he suspected the brain
meningitis was the doctors fear
and he ordered an ambulance from Belvidere
my father got home as it pulled away
completely unaware what happened that day

He had just finished his morning shift
and got home early as he had caught a lift
mother insisted that he shouldn't be told
he had a new job which was scarce as gold
and if he stopped work and rushed to her side
he'd be jobless tomorrow like most on the Clyde
so he left us with a neighbour then made his way
to Belvidere Hospital that wasn't far away

My mother went through all sorts of tests
x-rays and headscans and examining her breasts
the good news that there was no meningitis
or polio or tonsils or any other militis
the bad news was that she had tuberculosis
highly infectious and it came in doses
mother would be in hospital for an extended stay
and it wasn't too long before they took us away

My father as I see it had a difficult choice
stay in employment or look after his boys
we couldn't afford another job to be lost
and he had to keep it no matter the cost
there was no such things as creches or nannies
their parents were dead so we had no grannies
they said I was too young to look after the others
so it was off to a home for me and my brothers

My father was a typical Glasgow man
he'd hide his emotion whenever he can
he'd show no love and was oblivious to pain
but I know he cared just the same
we were taken away by an order of nuns
and I saw him weep at the loss of his sons
the only time in my life I ever I saw him cry
we only shook hands when I watched him die

When we got to the home they split us up
gave us some clothes and a wee plastic cup
it was the nursery for Pat as he was a wean
I don't think I ever saw him again
into the infants went Jim and Mick
I was left on my own and felt quite sick
I had to put on a shirt and a bib and brace
and I already knew I hated that place

One thing that always stuck in my mind
was toilet training your own behind
irrespective whether you needed it or not
you were stuck on a pan and made to squat
you'd sit for ages for something to come
sticking your fingers up your bum
and you weren't allowed to flush it away
till it was confirmed that you'd been that day

After the toilets it was straight to bed
about quarter to seven someone said
I was put in a dormitory like a hospital ward
given striped pyjamas that tied with a cord
for the first time in my life I was on my own
my mother in hospital and us in a home
I cried myself into an uneasy sleep
but no one saw this wee fella weep

A few months had passed and I felt rotten
thinking foolishly that we'd been forgotten
I sat down and wrote my very first letter
asking my ma will she please get better
I missed her and da and brothers so much
wondering why nobody had been in touch
and much to my delight she sent a reply
she'll see me soon and she wouldn't die

About a week later my father came
he had had enough and was taking us hame
he had sorted it out with the lady next door
who made us her own and then some more
she looked after us until mother was well
and got me out from that home from hell
three months had passed that lasted a year
when mothers tests were proven all clear

It was a Saturday morning I remember the day
we were sent to the pictures for the matinee
we couldn't wait till the end of the show
so before the trailers we decided to go
we ran all the way didn't wait for a bus
and she was oot the windae waiting for us
I ran up the stairs calling her name
and got a slap from my da as I forgot the wean

I never asked questions and I don't know why
were we taken away should our mammy die
but a home was for bad kids or so we were taught
so what did we do wrong is my lasting thought
now I thank God and old Effie next door
for the only crime committed was we were poor
and I often think when I am alone
what happened to the children I left in the home

The Saturday Matinee at the Odeon Shettleston: 1955

BALLS

We played fitba till well after dark
in the street our Hampden park
with a cardboard box or a rusty old tin
or anything else from the midden bin
the lamposts were goals and provided the light
as we played our game into the night
many a great player made his name
in the back streets of Glasgow playing this game

Now and again it was a tanner ball
playing keepy up against a wall
bouncing this ball off our head
playing records till ready for bed
some of the lads could go on all night
not stopping for tea or even a bite
they could go on and on and never stop
and never once would the little ball drop

There was a another game played by the girls
who portrayed completely different skills
bouncing the same wee tanner ball
two at a time against the wall
through their legs and behind their back
and only the girls had the knack
with buckled shoes no Reebok Kickers
their dresses tucked in their navy blue knickers

We somehow went to separate schools
the catholics and proddies and different rules
they brought us up to take a side
Celtic or Rangers but the never the Clyde
it was in the playground they set the scene
if you were orange or if you were green
to remain impartial you hadn't a hope
if it wasn't King Billy it was the Pope

There we played with a much bigger ball
that was made of rubber an orange an all
bouncing wildly all over the place
could cover your ears if it hit your face
in and out of the bicycle sheds
disturbing the girls that were playing beds
and *three and in* wasn't much fun
for playtime was over before it begun

Children playing in the back court with a wee tanner ball

The continental ball came to town
made of plastic cost half a crown
with polka dots and as light as a feather
you could play a game in any weather
no wonder continentals could bend a ball
with the outside of the foot around the wall
it would change direction in mid flight
the goalie gone left and the ball gone right
ten half time and twenty one the winner
and it would be the same again after dinner

The bladder is what Glaswegians call
the old fashioned leather ball
like a giant haggis tied up with a lace
a size five was commonplace
when it rained it weighed a ton
and up the wing you're expected to run
in old leather boots that were full of nails
on a muddy pitch after the gales

My Primary School – St. Michaels, Parkhead

Girls in the playground of St. Michaels, circa 1960

It was an honour to play for the school
fifteen lads made up the pool
there were no subs in our day
if you weren't picked you didn't play
I got my chance when I was ten
only because we were short of men
I was given a strip that had a hole
and with borrowed boots I scored a goal
it was the recognition that came my way
that shaped the person I am today

THE LOWLAND GAMES

Scotland is famed for its Highland Games
though an alternative came from Glesga hames
there was no Highland gathering for us to meet
so we met in our arena down in the street
and oot the windae was a grandstand view
for all to enjoy and not just the few
so get yourself ready and adjust your seats
for the Lowland Games in Glesga streets

Always a favourite was hide and seek
and if you were het you weren't to peek
you'd close your eyes and count to ten
catch them all then start over again
kick the can was a similar game
where you sought the players just the same
and if you got caught you couldn't play
till the can was kicked then you'd run away

The street about 1970. By this time the tenants had regenerated the front gardens.

The girls played hopscotch on drawn out beds
hopping and skipping and using their heads
pushing the peever only using their feet
into the numbered boxes chalked in the street
they played at ropes whilst singing their song
but had to caw when things went wrong
and the same songs were sung if you recall
as they bounced their balls against the wall

Each girl had a book and collected scraps
always changing doublers to fill in gaps
pictures of cherubs and angels with wings
pixies and elves and Queens and Kings
there was chinese ropes of elastic bands
straddling and jumping not using your hands
they played with a peerie or a whip and top
whipping furiously so it wouldn't stop

The first mode of transport for every young man
was the guidie made from the wheels of a pram
and an orange box on a plank of wood
and a rope to steer it if you could
we would make a girdie from a bicycle wheel
without the spokes a ring of steel
we would run for miles hitting this ring
before we learned how to turn the thing

We made bows and arrows from garden cane
a deadly weapon in the hands of a wean
peashooters and slings and the potato gun
forerunners of the weapons still to come
we played at dodgy with the tanner ball
and died as soldiers in dead man's fall
we played at rounders on the chalked out base
if you stood to close you'd get a bat in the face

There was no gold cup and no silver shield
no prizes of money from the very well heeled
there was no lap of honour or victory roll
just a pat on the back when you scored a goal
the Lowland games were all played for fun
sport to be enjoyed when we were young
we learned about life and what was right
down in the street The Stadium of Light

AHH-LEAVIOOO

This game was by far the best
stood head and shoulders above the rest
everyone could play and I've counted fifty
all fleet of foot and a wee bit nifty
they hung out their windae's in every hame
watching their children playing this game
the whole street turned out and we put on a show
the best game in town is ahh-leaviooo

The game was played in the middle of the street
between the lamposts where we used to meet
imaginary lines were the poles apart
and all behind one before we could start
the width of the street was almost as wide
as the length we'd run to the other side
but you had to get past the biggest guy
whose job it was to stop you going by

The game would start when he called out a name
and normally he picked on the smallest of wean
this would never present too much of a test
now there would be two to verse the rest
all the smaller kids were easy to catch
but they gradually got bigger and more of a match
he then called out my name and it was me to go
this was my chance for ahh-leaviooo

Well I steadied myself behind the line
watching the main man all the time
he was strategically placing his troops
encouraging them not to stand in groups
it was then that I spotted the gap
and went like a greyhound out of the trap
the big fella was smart and very aware
for he was the greyhound and I was the hare

Well I easily went past the first two kids
pushed them aside as if they didn't exist
then a wee girl who had plenty of nerve
was completely flatfooted by a body swerve
but this had forced me to go a bit wide
and into a garden on the right hand side
during the war they were made open plan
cut down the railings for the smelting man

Well I ran like mad keeping close to wall
I was almost there about past them all
then I saw in the corner of my eye
the biggest of guys letting fly
he came charging like a raging bull
I nearly wet myself but I stayed cool
I pulled on the brakes and suddenly froze
and he went flying past straight up a close

Those in the windae's started to cheer
as the imaginary line came ever near
they started jumping at the other end
and I was everybody's new best friend
I hopped and skipped over the line
and turned around the victory mine
I raised my arms in a triumphant show
and then I shouted Ahh-leaviooo

This was the signal for them all to run
and I stood back and watched the fun
I don't how many but there was a lot
running like mad not to be caught
for this was the purpose of the game
get past the catchers and go again
and I stood there bursting with pride
as most of them reached the other side

The big guy re-grouped and counted his men
then called out a name once again
now this was repeated till all were caught
and it lasted for ages more often than not
sadly these games are a thing of the past
despite being free and built to last
the kids of today will never know
the pleasure playing Ahh-leaviooo

THE FUNERAL

There was one visitor that we would dread
Bones the undertaker collecting the dead
the bereaved home was easy to find
it lay behind by a customary white blind
it was a common sight in Glesga streets
a grieving family behind ghostly sheets
pictures and mirrors all turned to the wall
for there was no reflection to be seen at all

The house of death kept an opened door
for a service at home the night before
people the deceased hadn't seen in years
drinking his health with a couple of beers
for here he lay there was no chapel of rest
his hands clasped firmly across his chest
a rosary and bible for his soul to save
the only possessions he'd take to his grave

He had died the previous Saturday night
his head in the oven without a light
he may have been drunk we'll never know
but the signs of decay were beginning to show
he had cotton wool instead of teeth
some up his nose and more underneath
he was decomposing and was starting to smell
though some old eedjit thought he looked well

The mourners were summoned if you please
for a few words to be said on bended knees
around the corpse the family would pray
before they came to take him away
the death mask appeared to frown
as the undertaker screwed him down
his sons were bearers thankfully not often
and onto their shoulders they hoisted the coffin

They carried him carefully down the stairs
out of the close and into the hearse
on top of the casket lay a family wreath
with another coffin concealed underneath
off slowly to church respectful in mind
for the grieving family walking behind
overnight before God a ritual for the dead
the first time in chapel since the day he wed

The church was full for the requiem Mass
a show of respect from the working class
the parish priest in his robes of black
on behalf of God welcomed him back
he had been a sinner most of his days
but before he died he repented his ways
a chancer and a wide boy to say the least
all was forgiven and blessed by the priest

The bereaved with great dignity and grace
took the departed to his resting place
into the cemetery to the family plot
where all his ancestors were left to rot
and they were listening underneath
to the last few prayers whispered in grief
will he get to heaven God only knows
in the name of the father and of the son . . .
                           and in the hole he goes

GOING MESSAGES

It was a June night if I remember
masquerading as mid December
the wind and rain was belting it down
over a grey and miserable Glesga town
a group of boys huddled in the close
blowing into their hands that had almost froze
then out of a window there came a shout
Davy will ye go to shops I can't get out

I wondered why I had been drawn
but I looked around my mates had gone
they saw her first tight fisted Jenny
apparently still owns her very first penny
but I was brought up to never to say no
though I wished I could tell her where to go
to send you to the shops on a night like this
really was taking the gypsy's kiss

I went up the stairs to an opened door
where she stood barefooted on the wooden floor
she had a cigarette dangling from her lips
her hair in curlers with her hands on her hips
her baby doll nightie looked out of place
on a bag of bones with a skeletal face
and the wrinkled stockings on skinny pegs
failed to hide her corned beef legs

She gave me some money wrapped in a note
be careful she said *that's all I've got*
and go to Johnny's and not to the hut
though the latter was closer and wasn't shut
this I found somewhat strange
twice the distance in the pouring rains
I was also taught to do as I was told
so off I went into the freezing cold

Ran all the way with no cap or coat
got to the shop and gave Johnny the note
he put on his specs and read into himself
then took a package down from the shelf
screwed up the note and chucked it away
gave me tuppence change my probable pay
I checked the date on the Victorian penny
but it had worn away there wasn't any

It was still raining and was getting dark
as I ran from the shop towards the park
for shelter keeping close to the wall
my package tucked in like a rugby ball
running down the imaginary wing
and 100,000 people started to sing
go on Davy I heard them cry
as I dived over the line to score a try

I must have tripped over my own two feet
for I felt myself hurtling towards the street
the newspaper pack was released from my care
and in slow motion flew through the air
It went higher and higher while spinning round
then slowly descended to the ground
the parcel burst open scattering its load
a dozen sanitary towels lay on the road

My hands and knees were covered in blood
and all the towels were caked in mud
I was fortunate as the traffic was light
as I must have been an sorry sight
scrambling around in the dirt
stuffing these things down my shirt
thinking hard how I would explain
de-sanitised towels in the pouring rain

Got myself home and like a fool
I tried to clean the cotton wool
but that only made things worse
and this is when I learned to curse
so I folded them neatly in rows of two's
and wrapped them up in the Daily News
gave her the parcel and didn't say
I kept the tuppence and ran away

'Five Boys' Chocolate (named after us)
(Picture reproduced courtesy of Cadbury Ltd)

THE MIDDEN

The cleansing motor disturbed the night
its headlights flashing and burning bright
roaring loudly it would waken the dead
never mind the neighbours who were all in bed
the midden men who just started their shift
were all on the backplates catching a lift
carrying wicker baskets on their backs
there was nothing hygienic as refuse sacks

Once a week they visited the street
through the closes in their dirty feet
it had just been washed with utmost pride
with a pipe clay border on either side
some wee woman on her hands and knees
scrubbing the close with relative ease
the woman's job cause her man couldn't cope
with a scrubber a pail and carbolic soap

The Midden Man

For whatever reason they came at night
and wore a helmet that provided the light
in the darkness the little lamp glowed
and lit up the middens that overflowed
they made a noise and chased the cats
and always wary of visiting rats
they tucked their trousers inside their socks
certainly not a job for kilted jocks

Into the baskets they tipped the bin
closing their eyes to the stuff that went in
including dogs and cats that recently died
wrapped in a parcel and poorly tied
there was no wheely bins or plastic bags
no protective clothing over their rags
no perspex goggles or protective mask
and very little pay for this hideous task

Middens were magnets during the day
to all the kids that went out to play
be it hide and seek or kick the can
or running away from the bogey man
jump on the bins then climb on top
to dreep off the dyke a six foot drop
then just for badness we thought was fun
we'd set light to the midden and watch it burn

One pastime that was filthy and mucky
was looking in middens for a lucky
through all the backs we'd search the bins
the dead dogs the cats and the empty tins
from bin to bin we'd search for hours
for a quality of rubbish better than ours
now and again we would strike it rich
a broken toy and a head that would itch

Our search will take us to older schemes
into their backs a theatre of dreams
washhouses and middens came up trumps
located together formed ideal jumps
there we would play daredevil games
follow the leader on jumps with names
the Duke and the Royal and the Devil's leap
and the wall of death for us to dreep

The middens provided a source of wealth
though never considered our state of health
did they also give us the scarlet fever
the scabies or polio or even diphtheria
they provided the arena for the jumps
a few cuts and grazes and a couple of bumps
and Mother's advice given completely free
if you break your legs don't come running to me

Children playing in the back court

MY AUNT CISSIE

I have told you of a home let me tell of another
only this story is told on behalf of my mother
her mother had died when she was a tot
of an unknown disease that she had caught
now she like us had a family of five
three brothers and two sisters and barely alive
they lived in the Calton near the Saracens Head
in a two roomed flat with a recessed bed

My mother was two when her mother died
aged about forty unless granda lied
her sister Cissie was a couple of years older
and a clever child at least thats what they told her
her brothers were in the army and had flew the nest
between the wars and no time for a rest
her father had a job in some sort of home
so she and her sister were a lot on their own

An old auntie looked after them now and again
of no blood relation which was common then
this was fine for a number of years
till grandad became fonder of his daily beers
for every day he would go for a drink
and if the girls complained he would cause a stink
he would stay in the pub till half past nine
then take home two screwtops and a bottle of wine

By the time the girls were seven and nine
they were out on the street most of the time
in and out of alleys and standing in doors
and when it rains in Glasgow it only pours
dinner was quite often a bag of chips
and the salt would sting their chapped lips
the wind and the rain and the winter chill
all took their toll when mother took ill

She was complaining about a pain in her ear
and got took to the clinic that was relatively near
they gave her eardrops then stuffed cotton wool
and gave her a note to stay off of school
but a few days later the pain got worse
and she was seen again by a visiting nurse
and my grandfather knew by the look on her face
that mothers illness was a hospital case

She was rushed to a hospital the other side of town
with nothing as much as a dressing gown
they discovered a mastoid in her inner ear
and their course of action was very clear
they decided to operate straight away
very doubtful if mother would last the day
she was unconscious and in great pain
there is nothing worse than a suffering wean

They removed the growth from inside her head
then took her back to her hospital bed
what loosely could be described as intensive care
the sick children of Glasgow reluctantly share
she was a very sick girl to say the the least
and this is confirmed when blessed by a priest
she was very weak and barely alive
and it was very doubtful if she'd survive

On several occasions she approached death's door
in and out of consciousness for a week or more
but slowly but surely she started to fight
and at the end of the tunnel appeared some light
she was taken out of the intensive care
to another wing she didn't know where
her eating improved and she got stronger
though her stay in hospital was getting longer

This was presenting a problem to granda Mick
his youngest daughter being long term sick
with the hospital being so far away
there was no way to visit every day
with Cissy at home and still at school
him at work and his schedule full
he had no wife and was on his own
it was an inconvenience with Cissy at home

Now the hospital which my mother was in
had what they called a healthy wing
this was for children taken into care
and also for orphans in need of a prayer
now Mick could kill two birds with one stone
one daughter in the hospital and one in the home
now they could be together with one and other
and well looked after with minimum bother

Well it seemed a good idea at the time
the two girls together should work out fine
with Cissy near hand and if the hospital let her
could look after her sister till she got better
now this worked out well and was quite a treat
and mother was quickly back on her feet
and the two girls longed for the day
when they could get home and go out to play

Mother was in hospital for a year and a half
and she only got better thanks to the staff
it was they who decided she could go home
and she wanted to tell Cissy on her own
she ran all the way to the healthy block
so excited she could hardly talk
the short journey didn't take long
but when she got there Cissy had gone

She was never to see her sister again
she was only eight and Cissy was ten
and her father never did relate
when questioned about his daughters fate
she was in better hands was all he gave
and he kept this secret till he went to his grave
my mother at writing is seventy eight
will we ever find Cissy or is it far too late

Granda Mick (right) with the lodger 'Geordie'

THE BIKE

I was thirteen and had never owned a bike
and could only dream of what it would be like
the kids in the street were all out on theirs
and I was watching from up our stairs
then one of the neighbours gave me a shout
to call in and see him when I was going out
I went down the stairs and he opened the door
and he pushed this bike across the floor

Would you like it son he casually said
Its been lying here since we've been wed
the wife's having a baby sometime in June
and I am clearing out the baby's room
I nodded gratefully and took it away
this I said was my lucky day
it had only one brake and a rusty chain
but I was really grateful to the new wee wean

Took it out the close and onto the street
the pedals clipped to my sandshoed feet
I felt great and was proud as punch
and even skipped my turn for lunch
I was showing off with all sorts of tricks
but I never knew the wheel was fixed
for I tried to stop and went over the bars
and onto the street head over arse

A few weeks later we had made a plan
to go camping with a couple of the gang
we would take our bikes and make the most
and cycle down to the Ayrshire coast
so on a Friday night we made our way
out of Glesga so drab and grey
bound for Saltcoats a cycling test
but got as far as Paisley Road West

We were cycling along as you do
three abreast when it should have been two
we never noticed the traffic cop
his hand held forward indicating stop
we weren't really going that fast
when we got to the copper and cycled past
mindlessly pedalling down the track
when the coppers whistle called us back

Where are you lot going he loudly cried
down the road I cheekily replied
he was totally impassive with no sense of humour
I knew straight away I had made a bloomer
he looked at me cold and straight in the face
and changed my mind about the human race
pulled out his pencil and pulled out his book
walked round the bike for a closer look

his book in hand he inspected my mount
pencil working overtime he started to count
five charges he gave me his best for the week
thats what you get for giving me cheek
we got another roasting then put on our way
and we were the punks that made his day
he never locked us up and I don't know why
those three desperados on the road to Dalry

I had never given it a great deal of thought
but after some months charges were brought
I received a summons and for my cheek
me and my da went before the beak
as I was a minor he was charged too
it made a change from signing the broo
we were found guilty and received a fine
three quid to be paid or we'd do the time

Well unknown to me it never got paid
and I don't know why he never said
on a Sunday morning just after four
there was a loud banging at our door
two big policemen how could they fail
to take this man and his boy off to jail
it was a fortnight in Barlinnie for my dad
approved school for me cause I was a lad

They frogmarched us down to the local nick
I got a roll and sausage about two inches thick
and a mug of cold tea that made me unwell
the one and only time I've been in a cell
who came to the rescue but dear old mum
who begged and borrowed the princely sum
what kind of person would I be today
if she didn't care and I was taken away

Tobago St. Police Station – The Local Nick

THE WEDDING

Dozens of people gathered round the close
including some guests in their best of clothes
all eagerly awaiting to see the bride
who was fidgeting nervously just inside
her father pacing around the room
still asking questions on her choice of groom
then up rolled the limo in shining black
that would take her away but won't bring her back

She looked so different in her dress of white
from the baby doll nightie the other night
her so called friends had dragged her out
on the streets of Glesga almost wearing nowt
it may have customary but it still was naughty
dressed up as a baby and carrying a potty
with this great dummy stuck in her mouth
in and out the pubs in Glesga south

They paraded her proudly as she'd got a man
and sung she was hard up and she kicked a can
everyone but her all thought it was funny
dressed up as a wean and collecting money
this was something she'd rather miss
a few pennies in the potty and a sloppy kiss
from unshaven men smoking and drinking
stale beer and roll-ups and breath that was stinking

The bride and her father were last to go
a wee drop of whisky to give him a glow
wellwishers formed a guard of honour
and to the more cynical another goner
hard up hard up the woman cry
and to this day I don't know why
they ran the gauntlet but it wasn't far
covered in confetti and got into the car

The kids in the street were going mad
for into his pocket reached her dad
he had a handful of money to chuck away
he'd been saving for months for this special day
through the open window his hand was raised
and all the kids got strategically placed
where you stood was always a gamble
out came the money that started the scramble

Ha'pennies an pennies an thrupenny bits
trying to catch some in your grubby mits
silver thrupennies disguised as tanners
and all the kids forgetting their manners
pushing and shoving on the ground
chasing the coins that were rolling around
down in the gutter for the last few pence
and at the time it seemed perfect sense

When the dust had settled after the stramash
we stopped and counted all of our cash
now tenpence ha'penny was a fair haul
four pennies a ha'penny and a tanner an all
my hands were cut and my knee was grazed
a small price to pay for the money raised
pulled up my socks in which I bled in
and went up the road to another wedding

The Scramble

Our Wedding 1972 – Annette and the Five Boys

Left to Right: Michael, David, Pat, Jim, Wee Alex at the front

FIRE

I have visions of when I retire
the pipe and slippers and the open fire
for then the cycle would be complete
for everyone had a fire down our street
and every home had a chimney or two
spitting out smoke from its filthy flue
polluting the air and creating the smog
a deadly combination the smoke and the fog

The fire was used like a second bin
if it could burn it went in
rubber or plastic or an empty box
shoes or boots or smelly socks
even potato peelings out of the sink
heaped on the fire creating a stink
the skins got baked with crispy edges
nowadays sold as potato wedges

We had what they call a back to back
an open range in matted black
and not only did it heat the place
it gave us hot water to wash our face
it also had a facility if you require
for cooking pots on top of the fire
you could wash and cook and heat your bum
and watch the flames dance up the lum

This was of course if we had the coal
or anything else that fitted the role
our bunker had been moved to the hall
and occasionally it held no coal at all
no shilling for the meter no gas or light
and no one to tap as money was tight
so anything we could find went on the fire
a burning boot and a smouldering tyre

My father was smart and knew what to do
for it was he who invented the barbecue
stacked shoes and boots like a funeral pyre
old rubber burning made the biggest fire
his frying pan ready he made the most
two eggs and a loaf and great French toast
very often we had this candlelit dinner
if marketed properly he was on to winner

Theres nothing better on a winters night
a blazing fire burning bright
all cuddled up nice and snug
competing for places on the tiny rug
outside it would be blowing a gale
the wind and rain and occasional hale
the flames would flicker on the fire
the swirling wind getting higher and higher

Then into the chimney it would come
blowing the smoke back down the lum
we never found it much of a joke
watching the telly through the smoke
or eating your dinner from a sooty dish
a plate of chips and a freshly smoked fish
coughing and spluttering until it cleared
and the next gust of wind always feared

At this time we'd call in the sweep
and into our loft he'd carefully creep
then onto the roof with his brush and pole
up on the chimney and shout down the hole
for he had to be careful and doubly sure
that he didn't sweep the chimney next door
for if he was out by less than a foot
them through the wall got covered in soot

More often than not or so it seemed
we'd no money to get the chimney cleaned
although the sweep was cheap to hire
it was cheaper still to set it on fire
a few old newspapers up the lum
light a match and watch it burn
out of the chimney the flames would roar
before the fire brigade came to the door

Round the back on the fifth of November
the biggest bonfire that I remember
for months we collected furniture and wood
and railway sleepers whenever we could
as high as the building we placed the guy
and watched him burn in the winter sky
bangers and rockets an annual treat
a wonder we never set fire to the street

When we'd get home we'd stink of smoke
and father would know before you spoke
we would totally deny being at a fire
but blackened eyes made you a liar
then he'd get us by the scruff of the neck
and put into the sink a nervous wreck
in front of the windae and completely nude
hiding our modesty if we could

After our bath it was straight to bed
they didn't believe a word we said
I always wondered why all the fuss
for all the kids lit fires not only us
although we were filthy from head to toes
it was the smell the fire left on our clothes
and they had to be washed and dried
for school tomorrow that's why we lied

The Glasgow chimney sweep

THE DROWNING

During the summer break from school
we wanted to go swimming in our local pool
we counted our pennies we hadn't enough
in Glesga they call it....tough
but it was a scorching summers day
and there was other water not far away
we lied to our parents and we tried to hide
we were going swimming in the River Clyde

We had climbed the slag the day before
a man made mountain from iron ore
from there we saw a sandy beach
just round the bend and easy to reach
our active minds did the rest
silver sands to compare with the best
even the river looked deepest blue
amazing what imagination could do

Whitevale Street public swimming baths

Walked up the river past Belvidere
bold as brass and free from fear
completely oblivious to the dangers ahead
and that one of the boys would soon be dead
half an hour later we were there
it wasn't Saltcoats but we didn't care
it had sand and water and even a tide
we were told never to swim in the Clyde

We scrambled our way down the bank
to the muddy beach where we almost sank
wee Pat got stuck so we gave him a hand
pulled him out of the mud and onto the sand
we looked at each other through eyes of fear
knowing perfectly well we shouldn't be here
the water was filthy and the whole thing messy
then someone shouted *last in is a Jessie*

The race was on and we started to strip
and one by one we went in for a dip
we had no trunks not even a towel
and into the water unbelievably foul
a river where no fish could survive
with leeches and rats to eat you alive
our heads bobbing from side to side
splashing the waters of the River Clyde

We got to the middle but didn't stay
for we felt the current pull us away
it was very difficult to keep afloat
the stench of the river down your throat
we had no choice but to turn around
and get our feet back on the ground
then up to our knees in slime and mud
covered in leeches sucking our blood

Grabbed our clothes and climbed the slope
and we tried to form a human rope
we never saw the jaggy nettles
cleverly hiding amongst the petals
screaming and shouting in demented fits
whilst trying to protect our dangly bits
we reached the top in a sorry state
cut to pieces and minus a mate

Dried ourselves off and started to dress
shirt outside in but couldn't care less
the mud was drying onto our skins
the nettles stinging our bleeding shins
our hair waffed of an oily pong
then we knew something was wrong
for only wee Pat had carried a comb
he wasn't here we thought he'd gone home

At first we thought he was kidding us on
for no one had saw where he had gone
we looked in the jaggies and also the hedge
then we looked down at the waters edge
for on the bank and out of the way
wee Pats clothes were where they lay
we ran down the hill calling his name
got back to the spot from where we came

Again we had a quick look round
refusing to believe that he may have drowned
we still thought he was taking the Mick
till a couple of the boys were physically sick
we stared at each other in disbelief
he really was gone in the waters beneath
all that remained was his pile of clothes
what to tell his mother God only knows

I ran to the steelworks to report our loss
and couldn't stop crying as I spoke to the boss
I was sobbing badly and shaking like a leaf
trying to speak through chattering teeth
he sat me down and took off his hat
and I told him slowly that we'd lost wee Pat
straight on the phone and without delay
the police and an ambulance were on their way

I took them down to where we played
and Pat's clothes were still where they laid
they looked up and down the river bank
the sergeant questioning on where he sank
we were all stunned and could hardly talk
fearfully trembling and overcome by shock
he looked into the river then shook his head
and knew perfectly well that Patrick was dead

Crowds started to gather on either side
waiting for the man who would drag the Clyde
mothers with babies wrapped in their shawls
little girls playing with their prams and dolls
courting couples out for a walk
whispering quietly when they talk
it really was a macabre sight
this carnival atmosphere on a summers night

The big policemen who rowed the boat
must have been sweating in his heavy coat
and the man in the back slung his hook
into the Clyde and it started to look
went up and down the river wide
searching the bottom of the filthy Clyde
he was a little man but very brave
as he took wee Pat from his watery grave

A pale bloated body floated to the top
and was pulled into the boat by the burly cop
it got covered quickly under a sheet
when all the women started to greet
sobbing out loud for our wee Pat
we showed no emotion we couldn't do that
us hard men frae Glesga we don't cry
he was only eleven and too young to die

THE ORANGE WALK

My youngest brother Alex.
This is his perception when my father took him to see the Orange Walk

Now I know I'm far too young to talk
but I'll make an exception for the Orange Walk
I am not very tall as I am not yet two
so I am on Dad's shoulders for a better view
but all I see is a sea of heads
baldies and bunnets and middle sheds
and hair styles purely designed to shock
I can't wait to see this orange walk

I can see what I think is a big parade
with all these banners being displayed
a soldier up front on his big white horse
a feather in his hat and pantaloon drawers
a young man followed leading a band
tossing this stick from hand to hand
he threw it upwards and heaven sent
the cheering got louder the higher it went

Then the biggest man with his massive drum
beating and banging from a big fat tum
his face as red as his nose was blue
the white of his bum was showing too
beating and banging from side to side
Boom Boom Boom his fathers pride
the backbone of the band and solid as a rock
but where the hell is that orange walk

Then came rows of men all playing flutes
looking grand in their toy soldier suits
with a spring in their step playing their tune
proudly marching through Glesga toon
the drummer boys bringing up the rear
beating their drums and playing by ear
when the music stopped they kept the beat
and made the pace walking down the street

Each of the bands had their own banners
carried by men with impeccable manners
with their white gloves and their bowler hats
and some carrying sticks like baseball bats
marshalls walking and defending the line
all in unison and in perfect time
orange sashes draped over their suit
there still no sign of that wandering fruit

The bands play louder and it's getting scary
completely drowning the bells of St Mary
singing and dancing a cacophony of noise
the Bridgeton loyal and the apprentice boys
jaked up on the Lanni and the VP wine
none of your Lambrusco or wines from the Rhine
and drinking beer and cider from plastic kegs
I still can't see an orange that has sprouted legs

We've walked up the street and round the block
and I am fed up looking for this orange walk
not a plum nor a banana not even an apple
but Dad saw a pear getting chased from the chapel
there was plenty nuts and plenty fruitcakes
that wanted to fight a bunch of grapes
who were booing and jeering in rival mock
I don't think I'll ever see that orange walk

Perhaps when I am older I will understand
about the procession and about the band
and why some people find it annoying
Orangeman celebrating the battle of the Boyne
so what if a footballer goes to mass
or blesses himself touching the grass
in this day and age does it really matter
what happened years ago across the watter

Glasgow would be a far better place
if we only listened to each others case
for aren't we all Jock Tamson's bairns
from Bridgeton the Gorbals or Newton Mearns
in a divided city where they walk alone
one lot on the streets and the rest at home
if those of influence could only take stock
then we all might see that Orange walk

The Orange Walk leaving St Enoch Square

MY FIRST KISS

Football had finished by the end of May
and Saturday became a very long day
our boring lives needed some enhancing
so someone suggested we go to the dancing
this was quite novel and we hadn't a clue
about twists or cha-chas or whatever you do
it could have been a tango or even the ballet
so we put on our best togs and went to the Palais

we got there early as doors opened at two
and we made our way to the end of the queue
it was four deep and stretched over the hill
there was hundreds of kids all dressed to kill
we had on our winklepickers and Italian suits
a far cry from our denims and welly boots
some had short trousers that openly displayed
the ring on their legs the wellies had made

The Dennistoun Palais

To the girls this was more than a game
the highlight of the week that's why they came
there was far more girls joined the queues
in their chiffon dresses and whitened shoes
though some were getting so much bolder
short skirts and make up and looking older
their hair was solid stuck with lacquer
and everyone of them looked a cracker

We paid our shilling and went into the hall
where all the young bucks stood against the wall
the girls danced round their bags on the floor
just like they danced the week before
they all seemed so grown up and knew what to do
for me this experience was completely new
I was more comfortable playing in the street
for I was the owner of two left feet

We went to a bar and bought a coke
and in a dark corner we sneaked a smoke
one fag between four so we each had a limit
that's three drags each and then we'd bin it
we finished our drink and went for a walk
and watched some girls rocking round the clock
I caught this girl with a seductive glance
but I daren't ask her if she would like to dance

Apparently it was customary to wait till the end
and catch the last dance with you and a friend
and as the girls normally danced in two's
you hadn't spent a penny so you'd nothing to lose
it was our intention to see them hame
even before you knew their name
get a winch and a cuddle down in the close
and a bit of heavy petting under her clothes

I continually gave this girl the eye
every time that I passed her by
this gradually progressed into a stare
it was becoming obvious but I didn't care
I wanted to dance her before it was to late
so I asked my pal if he fancied her mate
he gave me the nod so we went onto the floor
the music getting played slower and slower

I tapped her shoulder and asked her to dance
and this was the start of the briefest romance
we danced a moonie and got real close
cheek to cheek when I stood on her toes
we danced together hardly moving our feet
gently rocking to the music's beat
stars were sparkling on the ceiling above
and there and then I was falling in love

It was then it happened my first kiss
I never dreamed it could be like this
things were happening I can't describe
funny feelings deep inside
she looked into my eyes then closed her own
and I felt myself turning to stone
she placed her lips on top of mine
and I drunk a cup of the sweetest wine

The music had finished but we held our embrace
then the lights went on for something taking place
completely oblivious in the middle of the floor
mouths locked together demanding more
she caressed my lips with her tongue
very experienced from one so young
at last we stopped and came up for air
my eyes nipping from her lacquered hair

I glanced over her shoulder and onto the stage
there was a group of boys all of my age
nothing on Earth could tear us apart....
except the yo-yo competition that was about to start
you should have seen the look on her face
as I jumped onto the stage and got the last place
I pulled out my yo-yo and quite the thing
at the end of my finger secured the string

It was less than a minute after our snog
when I was on stage *walking the dog*
me and my yo-yo doing our stuff
it became quite obvious she'd got the huff
though it was her I was trying to impress
she turned away as she couldn't care less
my life would never be the same
and to this day I don't know her name

AFTER SCHOOL

I left school in sixty three
with a certificate that meant nothing to me
Dad wanted me in the building trade
pick up a trowel and you've got it made
better conditions and bigger pays
don't be a labourer all of your days
if you're a tradesman you've a job for life
and you won't have trouble supporting a wife

Don't be like me with five kids as well
in and out of work living in hell
his plans for my future were rather grim
second rung on the ladder one up from him
In the situations vacant in the Evening News
there were hundreds of jobs for me to choose
plumbers sparks brickies plenty that night
but none for labourers Dad was right

The building trade just couldn't be beat
they were building houses street after street
Castlemilk Easterhouse all over the place
sprawling estates without a face
the Glasgow I knew was being torn apart
the people their homes so close to my heart
shipping them out from where they were bred
out of the old slums to new ones instead

I did not share my fathers thought
contrary to what I was taught
I really risked a smack to the head
if I dare disagree with what he said
I didn't want to work on a site
I knew from school that it wasn't right
they tried to turn me into an engineer
rammed down my throat in the final year

They gave me a test I was expected to pass
I failed miserably bottom of the class
if I was to survive outside of school
I'd need to use my head and not a tool
a chef was what I really wanted to be
I could join the navy and be a cook at sea
but I constantly lived in fear
if my pals knew of my choice of career

A nancy boys job they would all agree
I'd as well be a fairy on top of a tree
if they found out and I would take some stick
a hard man frae Glesga should be laying brick
I had definitely made up my mind
that I wasn't the building kind
but I think I needed another look
there was no way I could become a cook

I went to the job centre we called it the broo
with dozens of others we formed a queue
the place was smelly and full of smoke
we stood in the line and never spoke
you didn't seem to have any choice
you took your turn with the rest of the boys
an apprentice joiner for the lad before me
now it was my turn I was soon to see

An office boy or shovelling muck
it was all down to lady luck
there was nobody there to give advice
to choose a career would have been nice
would it be cushy or would it be hard
totally dependent on the turn of a card
my whole life and what I would do
being determined by my place in the queue

THE CHALLENGE

Now the twentieth century has come and gone
my visions of the future were completely wrong
I had thought we would be walking in space
rockets on our backs being commonplace
I had dreams of a world free from disease
where we all had money that grew on trees
a world of no prisons where all would be free
and no homes for the children who were poor like me

Alas this fantasy is not to be
and our children are poorer I think you'll agree
they have their computers and the internet
and a million channels on their TV set
but the kids are prisoners in their own homes
and only talk to each other on mobile phones
virtual reality is the theme of the day
oh how I wish they would go out to play

Let us go forward some thirty years
and the year 2030 suddenly appears
it is hard to imagine what we cannot see
and we have no idea where the world will be
or even if man will still exist
or his arse goodbye was the last thing he kissed
it's a long time looking forward and thats a fact
but it is not very long when your looking back

So I would like to challenge the kids of today
to do as I have done based on Y2K
so open your eyes and have have good look
the people and places to put in your book
observe your world with an open mind
and take note on whatever you find
and in a few years time in another age
put down your thoughts on an open page

Only when this is done you may compare
your world with mine for all to share
go out there and prove me completely wrong
and that you were having fun all along
and if you are successful despite my doubt
go out on the rooftops and start to shout
and challenge the children you have then
to do as we have done and do it again

The street in 2000 – The kerbs and street lights preserved for posterity

REFLECTIONS

Looking back some thirty years after
through the tears and behind the laughter
I have nothing but pleasant thoughts
those days gone by when we were tots
in adulthood I discovered we were poor
but now I wonder and I'm not so sure
we had riches that you couldn't measure
and caring parents for us to treasure

Although we lacked in material gain
we seemed to get there just the same
Father unemployed and always skint
and those more affluent making a mint
five growing boys to clothe and feed
but always attentive to their every need
we were poor but never deprived
for every Christmas Santa arrived

Winter for us was a very lean time
ironically named British mean time
it was getting dark by mid afternoon
the lights were going on in Glesga toon
our's had been cut off and we'd no gas or coal
the old man barred from collecting his dole
this was the sixties in the welfare state
it never reached us or it must have been late

Man had just made his first flight in space
and we had no coal in the fireplace
we had no electric to supply the heater
for foreign coins stuck in the meter
we hadn't a shilling to put in the gas
and ice was forming on each pane of glass
we all snuggled up and got nice and warm
and we accepted this as part of the norm

94

I've never had a day off in this school of life
and I still don't know the meaning of strife
we were brought up hard but always fair
taught to be thoughtful and always care
and taught good manners and to show respect
nowadays known as politically correct
we were rough and ready but we weren't wild
and fairly typical of a post war child

My story has no political intent
and if my poetry offends it isn't meant
I choose my words carefully and may impress
but poetry is the vehicle for me to express
for if this was in text it wouldn't be read
and nobody would hear a word I've said
not to use my verse would be such a crime
but it is time to alight this tramcar of rhyme

The tram is nearing the end of the track
it can't turn round for there's no way back
now all I can do is make time to reflect
and I hope I am what my parents expect
I shall pass my story to my sons and heirs
and hopefully they'll pass it on to theirs
we're on this earth only custodians of time
and purely passengers to the end of the line

Lindsay Publications

PO Box 812 Glasgow G14 9NP
Tel/Fax 0141 569 6060
ISBN Prefix 1 898169